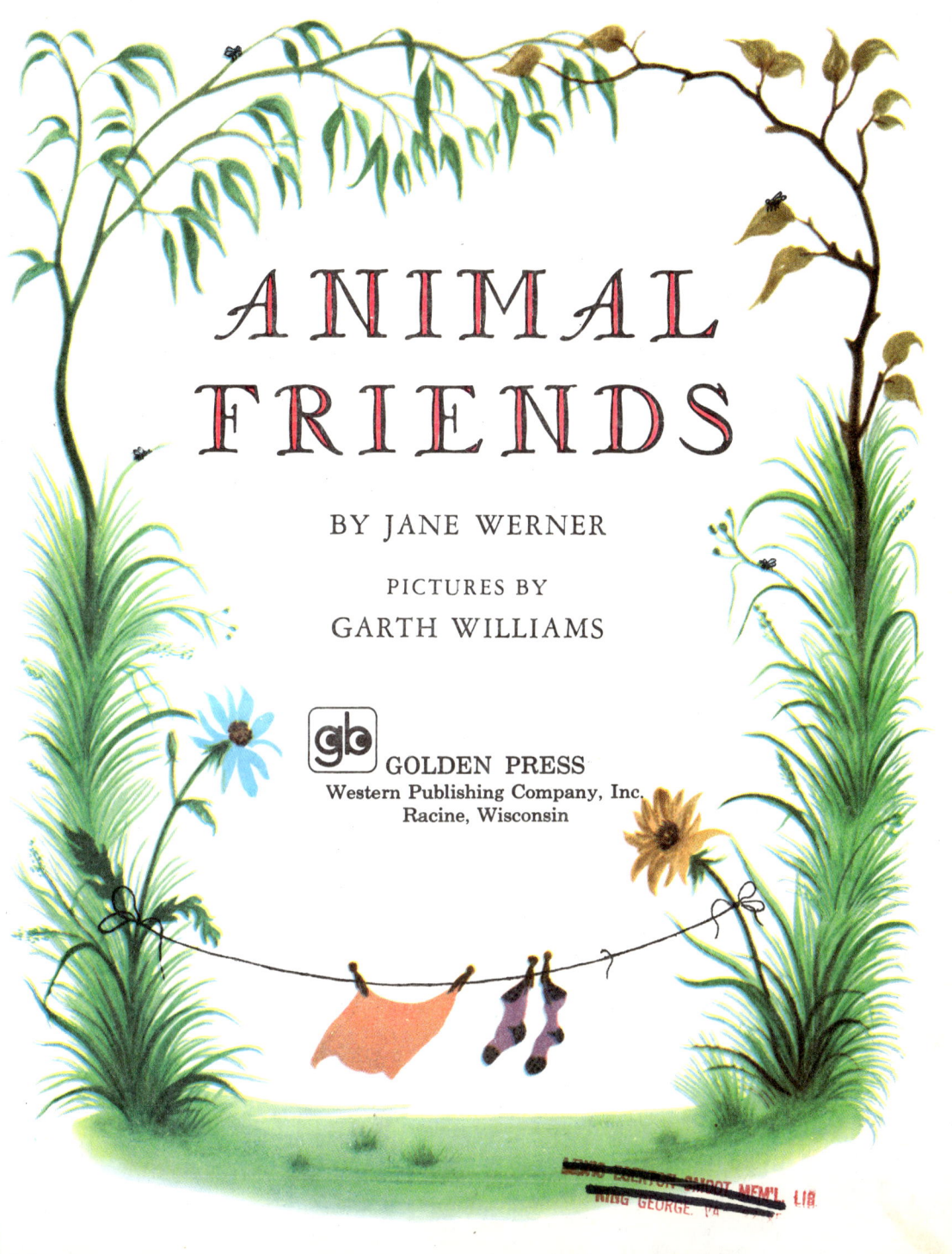

ANIMAL FRIENDS

BY JANE WERNER

PICTURES BY
GARTH WILLIAMS

GOLDEN PRESS
Western Publishing Company, Inc.
Racine, Wisconsin

GOLDEN, A LITTLE GOLDEN BOOK®, and GOLDEN PRESS®
are trademarks of Western Publishing Company, Inc.

AUTHOR AND ARTIST

Jane Werner has written, compiled and edited dozens of Golden Books of all sizes. Garth Williams' book illustrations have long delighted children. Among his recent favorites are BABY ANIMALS, BABY'S FIRST BOOK, HOME FOR A BUNNY, and THREE BEDTIME STORIES.

Copyright 1953 by Western Publishing Company, Inc.
All rights reserved. Produced in U.S.A.

Third Printing, 1975

ONCE upon a time, in a small house deep in the woods, lived a lively family of animals.

There were Miss Kitty and Mr. Pup, Brown Bunny, Little Chick, Fluffy Squirrel, Poky Turtle, and Tweeter Bird.

Each had his little chest and his little bed and chair, and they took turns cooking on their little kitchen stove.

They got along nicely when it came to sharing toys, being quiet at nap times and keeping the house neat. But they could not agree on food.

When Miss Kitty cooked, they had milk and catnip tea and little bits of liver on their plates.

Pup didn't mind the liver, but the rest were unhappy.

They didn't like any better the bones Pup served them in his turn. Nor Bunny's carrot dinners, or Tweeter's tasty worms, or Turtle's ants' eggs, or Squirrel's nuts.

When Bunny fixed the meals, she arranged lettuce leaves and carrot nibbles with artistic taste, but only Tweeter Bird would eat any of them. And when Tweeter served worms and crisp chewy seeds only Little Chick would eat them.

And Little Chick liked bugs and beetles even better. Poky Turtle would nibble at them, but what he really hungered for were tasty ants' eggs.

Fluffy Squirrel wanted nuts and nuts and nuts. Without his sharp teeth and his firm paws, the others could not get a nibble from a nut, so they all went hungry when Fluffy got the meals.

Finally they all knew something must be done. They gathered around the fire one cool and cozy evening and talked things over.

"The home for me," said Mr. Pup, "is a place where I can have bones and meat every day."

"I want milk and liver instead of bugs and seeds," said Miss Kitty.

"Nuts for me," said Squirrel.

"Ants' eggs," yawned Turtle.

"Crispy lettuce," whispered Bunny.

"A stalk of seeds," dreamed Bird, "and some worms make a home for me."

"New homes are what we need," said Mr. Pup. And everyone agreed. So next morning they packed their little satchels and they said their fond good-by's.

Squirrel waved good-by to them all. For he had decided to stay in the house in the woods.

He started right in to gather nuts.

Soon there were nuts in the kitchen stove, nuts in the cupboards, nuts piled up in all the empty beds. There was scarcely room for that happy little Squirrel.

The others hopped along till they came to a garden with rows and rows of tasty growing things. "Here's the home for me," said bright-eyed Brown Bunny, and she settled down there at the roots of a big tree.

Little Chick found a chicken yard full of lovely scratchy gravel where lived all kinds of crispy, crunchy bugs.

"Here I stay," chirped Chick, squeezing under the fence to join the other chickens there.

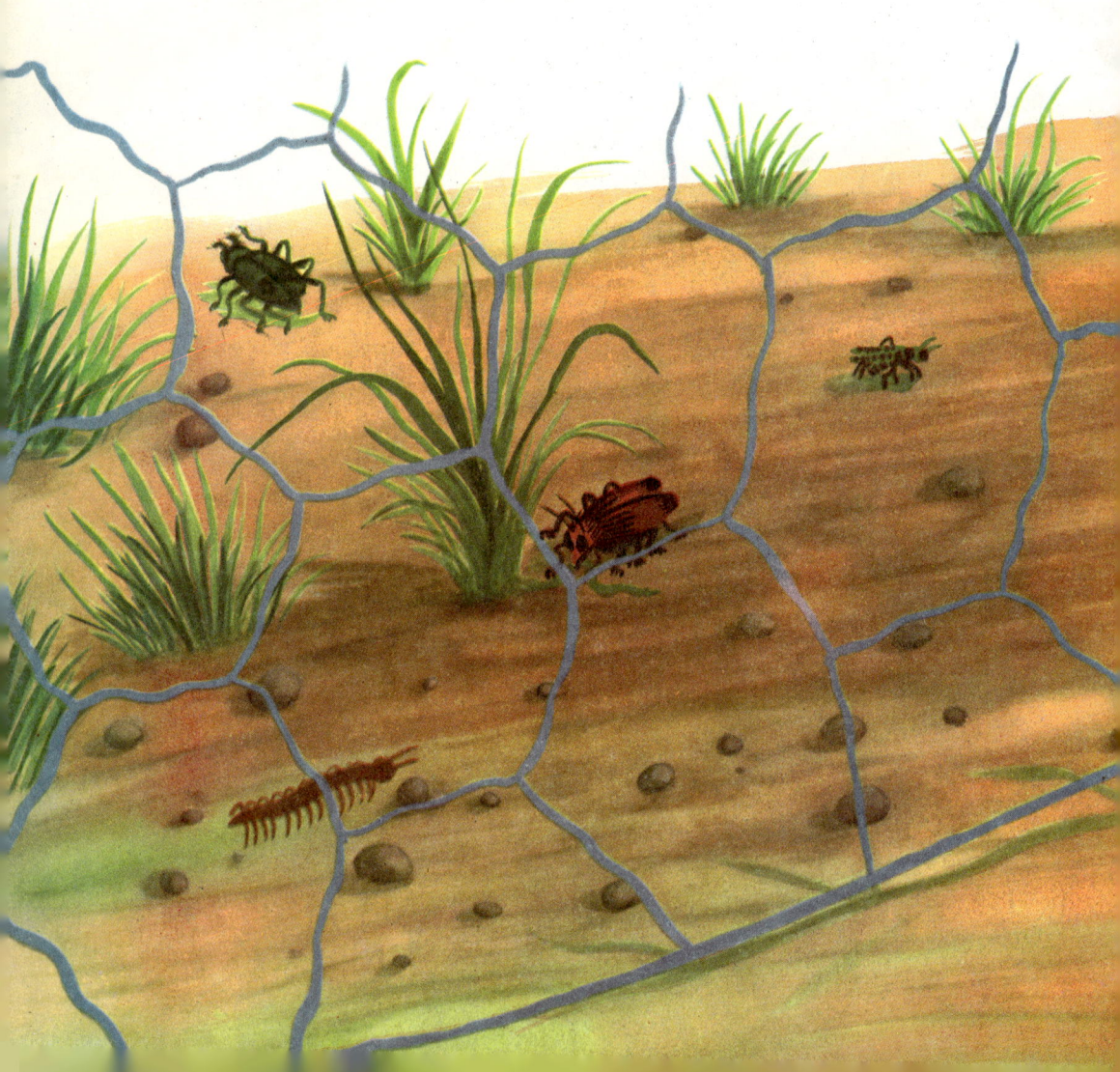

Poky Turtle found a pond with a lovely log for napping, half in the sun, half in the shade.

Close by the log was a busy, bustling ant hill, full of the eggs Turtle loved.

Tweeter Bird found a nest in a tree above the pond, where he could see the world, the seeds on the grasses, and the worms on the ground.

"This is the home for me," sang Bird happily.

Miss Kitty went on till she came to a house where a little girl welcomed her.

"Here is a bowl of milk for you, Miss Kitty," said the little girl, "and a ball of yarn to play with."

So Miss Kitty settled down in her new home with a purr.

Mr. Pup found a boy in the house next door. The boy had a bone and some meat for Pup, a bed for him to sleep in, and a handsome collar to wear.

"Bow wow," barked Pup. "This is the home for me."

That night each one said, as he went to sleep, "At last I've found the best home of all, the very best home for me."